GOD's MAN
KING DAVID

God's Man
King David

A Giant Print 40 Day Devotional

Mark Sundy

Xulon Press

Xulon Press
2301 Lucien Way #415
Maitland, FL 32751
407.339.4217
www.xulonpress.com

© 2017 by Mark Sundy

All rights reserved solely by the author. The author guarantees all contents are original and do not infringe upon the legal rights of any other person or work. No part of this book may be reproduced, stored in a retrieval system, or transmitted in any form or by any means without expressed written permission of the author. The views expressed in this book are not necessarily those of the publisher.

Scripture quotations taken from the New King James Version (NKJV). Copyright © 1979, 1980, 1982 by Thomas Nelson, Inc. Used by permission. All rights reserved. Printed in the United States of America.

Scripture quotations taken from the Holy Bible, New International Version (NIV). Copyright © 1973, 1978, 1984, 2011 by International Bible Society. Used by permission of Zondervan Publishing House. All rights reserved.

Scripture quotations taken from the King James Version (KJV) – *public domain.*

Scripture quotations taken from the Holy Bible, New Living Translation (NLT). Copyright ©1996, 2004, 2007 by Tyndale House Foundation. Used by permission of Tyndale House Publishers, Inc.

Scripture quotations taken from The Voice Bible Copyright © 2012 Thomas Nelson, Inc. The Voice™ translation © 2012 Ecclesia Bible Society. All rights reserved. Used by permission.

Scripture quotations taken from The Message (MSG). Copyright © 1993, 1994, 1995, 1996, 2000, 2001, 2002. Used by permission of NavPress Publishing Group. Used by permission. All rights reserved.

Scripture quotations taken from the Amplified Bible (AMP). Copyright © 1987 by The Lockman Foundation. Used by permission. All rights reserved.

ISBN-13: 9781545604595

Dedication

This book is dedicated *in memoriam* to my friend, Louis Constancio. Born February 18, 1971, promoted to eternity on February 24, 2017. It is amazing how one life can touch so many others. Louis touched all he came into contact with kindness and generosity. He loved life and life loved him. He was a father, a son, and a husband. Louis was a friend to everyone. He will be missed by so many on Earth. Though in Heaven, there is a big celebration of his homecoming. I thank God for you, Louis Constancio, and may God bless your family.

Table of Contents

Acknowledgements xi
Introduction. xiii
Day 1: God Seeks a Man after His Own Heart. 1
Day 2: David the King. 3
Day 3: Do All of God's Will 5
Day 4: Training for Reigning 7
Day 5: God Is with David 9
Day 6: David Honors the King's Authority. 11
Day 7: The Goliath Test 13
Day 8: David's Courage 15
Day 9: God Was David's Armor 17
Day 10: David Prepares for Battle 19
Day 11: David's Amazing Faith 21
Day 12: Seek First the Kingdom of God. 23
Day13: David Behaved Wisely 25
Day 14: David Becomes Leader of the
        Disenchanted 27
Day 15: David Refuses to Harm the Lord's
        Anointed. 29
Day 16: David and Abigail. 31

Day 17: David in the Army of Achish 33
Day 18: David Is Fair with His Soldiers 35
Day 19: King David Grew Stronger and Stronger 37
Day 20: David's Reign Begins. 39
Day 21: David Danced with All His Might 41
Day 22: God's Greatness. 43
Day 23: The Lord Preserves David 45
Day 24: David and Mephibosheth 47
Day 25: David and Bathsheba 49
Day 26: King David and the Prophet Nathan. 51
Day 27: God's Judgment on King David 53
Day 28: David Heartbroken at Absalom's Death 55
Day 29: Three Years of Famine. 57
Day 30: David's Song. 59
Day 31: David Numbered the People. 61
Day 32: David Advanced in Years. 63
Day 33: Adonijah Takes the Throne 65
Day 34: David Charges Solomon 67
Day 35: King David Dies. 69
Day 36: David's Soul Thirsts for God. 71
Day 37: David Repents with a Contrite Heart 73
Day 38: David Asks God for a Clean Heart 75
Day 39: David Walks in God's Truth 77
Day 40: Your Word I Have Hidden in my Heart . . 79
Conclusion. 81
Appendix: The Abigail Blessing. 85
About the Author 91

Acknowledgements

I am grateful to my daughter, Kristina Sundy Benton, and my son, Nathan Sundy, who make life a joy. To my two grandchildren, Hailey and Patton, who are my sunshine. To my father, Allen Sundy, and my mother, Mary Harrell Sundy, who were an inspiration to me. To Samantha Sundy, Gary Faulkner, Beverly Sundy, and Linda Sundy for their support.

I am grateful to the Father, the Son, and the Holy Spirit, the one and only true God—the Blessed Trinity for giving me the breath of life.

I would like to thank my sister, Rita Sundy Faulkner, for her caring support while I was working on this book.

I would also like to thank my two brothers, Randall Sundy and Steve Sundy, for their encouragement.

I would like to extend gratitude to Henry and Mary, Howard and Carolyn, Ralph and Jessica, Brenda and Steve, Freddy, Lou and Corina, Kathy and Arturo, Lupe, and Jacque for their prayers, grace, and loving compassion.

I would like to thank Trey Lancaster for our Bible discussions over lunch on Sunday's after church.

I owe my gratitude to a multitude of Christian Mentors, Teachers, Pastors, Prophets, Evangelists, and Sunday School Teachers who helped me in my walk with the Lord Jesus Christ.

I would especially like to thank Sr. Editor Dr. Larry Keefauver and Editor Pamela McLaughlin for all the hours they spent proofreading and editing the manuscript. Without you, this book would not have come to fruition.

A good book is always a team effort. Gratitude is expressed to the editors, typesetters, cover designers, printers, and all the others in the publishing business who made this book possible.

INTRODUCTION

This giant print, forty-day devotional is based on the life of God's man, David, who went from a simple shepherd boy to the king of Israel. Though not a perfect man, God called David a "man after His own heart."

Forty is a notable number in the Bible. Jesus fasted forty days before He was tempted by Satan (Matthew 4:1-2). Moses fasted for forty days and nights on the Mountain of God (Exodus 24:18). Israel wandered in the wilderness for forty years (Numbers 14:23). Goliath taunted Israel for forty days (1 Samuel 17:16). It rained forty days and nights during the Great Flood in Noah's time (Genesis 7:4). God gave Nineveh forty days to repent (Jonah 3:4).

The Bible says, "Draw near to God, and He will draw near to you" (James 4:8). To do this you must spend time with the Father and learn from the stories He has recorded for us in His Word to teach and guide us.

I encourage you to use this devotional in conjunction with God's Word and utilize the next forty days to draw near to God.

Fasting one day a week or even one meal a week will also help you draw near to God. However, fasting should not be attempted until you discuss it with and it is approved by your medical provider.

It's time to get excited because this forty-day devotional is going to bring you closer to God than you have ever been before. This forty-day devotional may be utilized at Lent as a preparation for the Easter season or by groups or individuals during any forty-day segment of time.

All you need is a desire to draw near to God!

Day 1

GOD SEEKS A MAN AFTER HIS OWN HEART

*The Lord has sought for Himself **a man after His own heart**, and the Lord has commanded him to be commander over His people, because you have not kept to what the Lord commanded you.* (1 Samuel 13:14 emphasis added)

Saul, the first king of Israel had received the Spirit of God when Samuel anointed him as king (1 Samuel 10:1, 9-10). However, God's patience with King Saul ran out when he was blatantly disobedient to God's instructions. The Spirit left Saul when God sent Samuel to anoint David as the next king of Israel. David was chosen because God saw within him a desire to continually draw closer to Him.

God is still seeking men and women who are after His heart.

Drawing Closer to God

Why would you want to draw near to God? (See James 4:8).

___

How are you to draw near to God? (See Hebrews 10:22).

___

What are some ways you can do this? (See Psalm 119:9-16).

___

Pray: *Heavenly Father, help me to choose to be obedient to Your precepts and develop a heart that continually seeks after Your heart. Show me how to draw closer and closer to You as I spend time in Your presence these next forty days. In Jesus' name I pray.*

Day 2

DAVID THE KING

Now the Lord said to Samuel, "How long will you mourn for Saul, seeing I have rejected him from reigning over Israel? Fill your horn with oil, and go; I am sending you to Jesse the Bethlehemite. For I have provided Myself a king among his sons." 1 Samuel 16:1)

David was the youngest of Jesse's eight sons. He was a simple shepherd who had spent many days alone in the fields with the sheep and his harp drawing closer and closer to God. He was only a young person when the prophet Samuel came to his father's house in obedience to the Lord's command. However, when Samuel explained to Jesse his true mission, Jesse didn't even think it necessary to call David in from the fields.

David's father judged David according to man's standards and the boy's outward appearance. He did not "look like a king."

**God sees our heart,
while men judge our outward appearance.**

Drawing Closer to God

What does Proverbs 27:19 tells you about your heart?
_____

What does Psalm 51:17 say God is looking for in our hearts? _____

In Matthew 12:34 Jesus said, "Whatever is in your _____ determines what you _____" (NLT).

Psalm 139:23-24 tells us we should ask God to what six things?
1. _____ me
2. _____ my heart
3. _____ me
4. Know my _____
5. See if there is any _____ ways in me.
6. _____ me in the way _____

Pray: *Heavenly Father, search my heart and show me what needs to be changed to conform to Your image. In Jesus' name I pray.*

Day 3

Do All of God's Will

And when He had removed him, He raised up for them David as king, to whom also He gave testimony and said, **"I have found David the son of Jesse, a man after My own heart, who will do all My will."** (Acts 13:22 emphasis added)

When God looked at David's heart, He saw a man who would do **all** His will. The only way David could know God's will was to seek an intimate relationship with God. Jesus said, "'You must love the Lord your God with **all** your heart, **all** your soul, and **all** your mind.' This is the first and greatest commandment" (Matthew 22:37-38 NLT emphasis added). David had learned this truth sitting in the fields watching over and defending his father's sheep.

God is looking for men and women who will do all His will.

Drawing Closer to God

Romans 10:10 says, "For it is by believing in your _____ that you are made _____ with God" (NLT).

Romans 12:2 says you can know God's will by:
_____

When Jesus said to love God with **all** your heart, soul, and mind, were there any exceptions to this command?
_____

So then when Jesus said **all** He meant _____!

Read 1 Samuel 13:13-14. What did King Saul do that caused God to remove him and replace him with David as king? _____

Pray: *Heavenly Father, help me to know and do **all** Your will. Show me how to love You with **all** my heart, **all** my soul, and **all** my mind as I seek to serve and obey You with **all** that is within me. In Jesus' name I pray.*

Day 4

TRAINING FOR REIGNING

So as David stood there among his brothers, Samuel took the flask of olive oil he had brought and anointed David with the oil. And the Spirit of the Lord came powerfully upon David from that day on. (1 Samuel 16:13 NLT)

David's "heart" training began while he was a shepherd caring for his father's sheep. He had submitted to his father, done his job with a willing and faithful heart, and learned to seek God's presence on a daily basis in order to survive and fulfill his duties.

Samuel anointing David as the next king was only the beginning of his journey. Now he was ready for the next phase of his training for reigning.

Being led and trained by the Spirit of God.

We can't fulfill our mission in life unless we have been trained and led by God's Spirit.

Drawing Closer to God

Romans 8:13-14 says we need to _____ by the Spirit and be _____ by the Spirit to be true _____ of God.

In John 16:13-15, Jesus told His disciples why they needed to be led by the Holy Spirit.
He will guide you into all _____.
He will tell you what is yet _____.
He will make what is of the Father _____ to you.

Pray: *Heavenly Father, I submit to and welcome Your discipline and training in order to carry out the assignment You have given me. Please send Your Holy Spirit to lead and guide me into Your truth. In Jesus' name I pray.*

Day 5

GOD IS WITH DAVID

At that very moment the Spirit of God left Saul and in its place a black mood sent by God settled on him. He was terrified. Saul's advisors said, "This awful tormenting depression from God is making your life miserable.... I know someone. ***I've seen him myself: the son of Jesse of Bethlehem, an excellent musician. He's also courageous, of age, well-spoken, and good-looking. And God is with him.***"
(1 Samuel 16:14-18 MSG emphasis added)

It is interesting to note that God already had a man in place among King Saul's servants who not only knew of David's music skills, but described him as "courageous, well-spoken, good-looking, and GOD IS WITH HIM." IT IS AMAZING THAT THIS SERVANT SOMEHOW RECOGNIZED THAT GOD WAS WITH DAVID.

**God was with David wherever he went.
Drawing Closer to God**

David went to the palace and faithfully served the present king. He was now in training for his eventual position as king. God placed him in King Saul's service so he could learn firsthand the duties and responsibilities of a king.

Many challenges would face David as he adjusted to palace life, but he always knew God was with him.

Read 1 Samuel 18:12-16 and 28-29.

Why was King Saul afraid of David?

___

Why did David have great success in whatever he did?

___

What did King Saul realize more and more about David?

___

Pray: *Heavenly Father, I ask You to be with me in the same way You were with David. In Jesus' name I pray.*

Day 6

DAVID HONORS THE KING'S AUTHORITY

So David came to Saul and stood before him.... and he became his armor bearer.
(1 Samuel 16:21)

Though he had been anointed by Samuel to be the next king, David honored the man God had currently placed in authority over the nation. David submitted to the king's authority, and even became King Saul's armor bearer. An armor bearer carried his leader's shield and was to help keep his leader safe in battle.[1] David was actually in training to move from being a shepherd of sheep to a military leader and then the king. He was training for reigning.

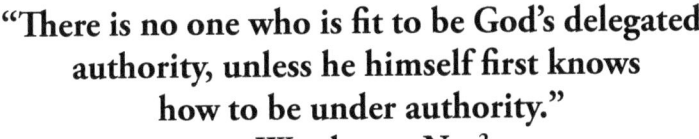

"There is no one who is fit to be God's delegated authority, unless he himself first knows how to be under authority."
– Watchman Nee[2]

---

[1] Terry Nance, *God's Armor Bearer*, p. 11
[2] *Spiritual Authority*, p. 115

Drawing Closer to God

Hebrews 13:17 tells us to:
_____

Why is it so important to honor authority?
_____

Romans 13:1 says we are to _____ to governing authorities because _____.

In fact, Romans 13:2 warns us if we rebel against those God has put in authority over us, we are actually
_____!

What does Romans 13:5 add to this?
_____

Pray: *Heavenly Father, I do not want to rebel against You in any way. Please help me submit to those authorities You have placed over me so I can become the leader You have called me to be. In Jesus' I pray name.*

Day 7

THE GOLIATH TEST

"I defy the armies of Israel this day; give me a man, that we may fight together." When Saul and all Israel heard these words of the Philistine, they were dismayed and greatly afraid. (1 Samuel 17:10-11)

The Philistines were an ongoing threat to Israel. When they gathered their troops to encroach on Israel territory, King Saul gathered his troops and they faced each other on opposite hills. The Philistines brought with them a champion, a giant named Goliath. In ancient times, rival forces would seek to cut down on causalities by choosing a champion to represent them. Goliath was an intimidating warrior who was over nine feet tall. This champion shouted taunts across the valley at the Israelite soldiers every day for forty days. In the Bible, "40" is the number of testing.

God was testing Israel through Goliath.

Drawing Closer to God

What was God's test for Israel through Goliath?
_____

Do you have a "Goliath" in your life? ___
Describe it: _____
Is God using this "Goliath" to test you? ___

Deuteronomy 8:2 says, "Remember how the Lord your God led you through the wilderness for these forty years, humbling you and testing you to prove your _____, and to find out whether or not you would _____ _____ _____" (NLT).

How did this help you understand why God might be testing you through your "Goliath" and what you need to change? _____

Pray: *Heavenly Father, grant me wisdom and understanding, and show me what I need to change in my life during this "Goliath" test. In Jesus' name I pray.*

Day 8

DAVID'S COURAGE

"Choose a man for yourselves, and let him come down to me. If he is able to fight with me and kill me, then we will be your servants. But if I prevail against him and kill him, then you shall be our servants and serve us." And the Philistine said, "I defy the armies of Israel this day; give me a man, that we may fight together." (1 Samuel 17:8-10)

When David heard the taunts of Goliath, he questioned why Saul and the army that served the living God had not stood against the pagan army. He volunteered to face Goliath as Israel's representative knowing God had delivered him from a lion and a bear in the past. "The Lord, who delivered me from the paw of the lion and from the paw of the bear, He will deliver me from the hand of this Philistine" (1 Samuel 17:37).

David's courage came from his faith in God.

Drawing Closer to God

Read 1 Samuel 17:34-36.
Why did David say he knew God would deliver him from the hand of Goliath?

_____

What did David write in Psalm 23:5 about God's provision from his enemies?

_____

Psalm 18:34 says _____ trained him for _____.

Psalm 18:35 says _____ was his _____

Psalm 18:39 says _____ armed him with _____ for battle.

Pray: *Heavenly Father, I ask You to grant me courage through my faith in You so I can face and defeat my Goliath. Remind me of the times You have provided all that I needed for victory in the past. In Jesus' name I pray.*

Day 9

GOD WAS DAVID'S ARMOR

> *David said to Saul, "'I'm not used to these things. How can I attack an enemy when I can't even walk?' So, he removed every bit of Saul's armor. He would fight the Philistine as he had fought those lions and bears."*
>
> (1 Samuel 17:39 VOICE)

King Saul sought to equip David with his own personal armor. David's weapons were those he had used in his role as a shepherd. He had become extremely accurate with his sling which was basically a pouch with two leather thongs. It was whirled rapidly and then one of the throngs would be released sending the stone toward a target without having to get right up next to it. Though he had not specifically trained as a soldier, David had learned the importance of strategically hitting an enemy in vulnerable, disabling spots on the body. This prepared him to face even an enemy with heavy body armor.

David believed his God would protect him.

Drawing Closer to God

In Psalm 23, David calls God his _____ because God _____ and _____ for him like David did his father's sheep.

David said the Lord's rod and staff brought him comfort.

What is the difference in a shepherd's rod and his staff?
_____

What was a shepherd's rod used for?
_____

What a shepherd's staff used for?
_____

In John 10:11, Jesus calls Himself our _____ _____.

Pray: *Heavenly Father, I believe You will protect me in every area of my life as I put my faith and trust in You. Thank You, Father God, for being my shepherd. In Jesus' name I pray.*

Day 10

David Prepares for Battle

Then he took his staff in his hand; and he chose for himself five smooth stones from the brook, and put them in a shepherd's bag, in a pouch which he had, and his sling was in his hand. And he drew near to the Philistine.
(1 Samuel 17:40)

The weapons David used were also symbolic. The number "5" stands for the grace of God. Proverbs 3:34 says God, "pours out His grace on the humble" (VOICE).

As a man that sought to serve God, the shepherd's staff David carried stands for humility. David was a young man of character whose confidence was in God, not his own skills as a soldier. His humility would eventually make him a great servant-leader beloved by his kingdom.

Humility is a trait we all need in our walk with God.

Drawing Closer to God

Why is godly humility so important in our quest to draw closer to God? _____

Psalm 25:9 says God _____ the humble in what is _____.

Proverbs 11:2 says with pride comes _____, but with humility comes _____.

Proverbs 15:33 says humility comes before _____.

In Matthew 23:12, Jesus said whoever exalts himself will be _____, but whoever humbles himself with be _____.

1 Peter 5:5 says we are to _____ ourselves in humility because God gives _____ to the _____.

Pray: *Father, help me develop the godly trait of humility so that I can be the leader You have called me to be. In Jesus' name I pray.*

Day 11

David's Amazing Faith

He [David] picked up five smooth stones from a stream and put them into his shepherd's bag. Then, armed only with his shepherd's staff and sling, he started across the valley to fight the Philistine. Goliath walked out toward David with his shield bearer ahead of him, sneering in contempt at this ruddy-faced boy. "Am I a dog," he roared at David, "that you come at me with a stick?" And he cursed David by the names of his gods. "Come over here, and I'll give your flesh to the birds and wild animals!" Goliath yelled. (1 Samuel 17:40-44 NLT)

David's amazing faith was openly displayed as he boldly approached the giant warrior Goliath. It was obvious to those all around them that David was putting actions to his words of faith after telling King Saul the Lord would deliver him from Goliath.

David's amazing faith was openly displayed.

Drawing Closer to God

Our lives clearly reflect our faith. Those around us can tell if we truly believe in the God we say we trust.

James 2:17 says if faith is not accompanied by _____ it is _____.

James 2: 18 says I will show you my faith by _____ _____.

James 2:24 says a person is justified by what he _____ not by just his _____.

Where do your actions tell others you have placed your faith and trust? _____

Do you boldly face the challenges in your life declaring God is your provision and protection? _____ Explain your answer.

Pray: *Heavenly Father, I ask You to show me how to develop this amazing faith in my life. In Jesus' name I pray.*

Day 12

SEEK FIRST THE KINGDOM OF GOD

*David said, "You come to me with a sword, with a spear, and with a javelin. But I come to you in the **name of the Lord of Hosts**, the God of the armies of Israel whom you defied. **This day the Lord will deliver you into my hand, and I will strike you and take your head from you.** " So, David prevailed over the Philistine with a sling and a stone."*
(1 Samuel 17:45-46, 50 emphasis added)

The story of David is not only literal, historical fact, it is full of revelation and wisdom for today. This story shows us how to arm ourselves with faith, humility, and the name of the Lord to defeat our giants and gain the victory. This can only be done if we seek first the kingdom of God and obey His ways.

If we seek first the kingdom of God, He provides everything we need for victory no matter what enemy we face.

Drawing Closer to God

David was obviously a seeker of God. Therefore, God's promises for deliverance, healing, salvation, and provision were his. These same promises are still available to seekers of God today and will lead us to overcome pain, sickness, infirmities, financial difficulties, bankruptcies, divorce, and addictions.

What was the first thing David declared as he approached the fully armed Goliath?

_____

What did he tell Goliath God was going to do?

_____

Pray: *Heavenly Father, I decree and declare* **victory** *in every area of my life. In Jesus' name I pray.*

Day 13

DAVID BEHAVED WISELY

> *And **David behaved wisely** in all his ways, and the Lord was with him. Therefore, when Saul saw that he behaved very wisely, he was afraid of him.* (1 Samuel 18:14-15 emphasis added)

Saul became afraid of David and tried to kill him by casting a spear at David, but David eluded him twice (1 Samuel 18:11).

> ***Saul** was afraid of David because the Spirit of the Eternal was with him but had left Saul. So, at last, Saul removed David from his presence, making him a commander over 1,000 men, hoping he would die in battle. But David went out to the battle and returned.* (1 Samuel 18:12-13 VOICE)

The Lord is with us when we behave wisely even when others act foolishly around us.

Drawing Closer to God

1 Samuel 18:5 says David went out wherever Saul sent him and behaved _____.

1 Samuel 18:30 says David behaved more _____ than all the other servants of Saul so that his name became _____.

Proverbs 16:20 tells us he who heeds the word wisely will find _____.

James 1:5 tells us if we lack wisdom all we have to do is _____.

Pray: *Heavenly Father, I ask You to give me Your wisdom from above that I may behave wisely in all my ways so that Your presence will be with me. In Jesus' name I pray.*

Day 14

DAVID BECOMES LEADER OF THE DISENCHANTED

And everyone who was in distress, everyone who was in debt, and everyone who was discontented gathered to him. So he became captain over them. And there were about four hundred men with him. (1 Samuel 22:2)

David became a leader over those on the fringe of society. Up until this point, David had been a servant: first to his father and then to King Saul. His leadership skills developed as he became a military leader, but now he needed to work with the disillusioned and turn them into mighty men for God.

God is able to use those disenchanted with this world system for the glory of His Kingdom.

Drawing Closer to God

David was now being called to influence the lives of others and build an army for God. We are also called to be a godly influence on those around us. We are all leaders in some aspect of our purpose in God's kingdom.

2 Corinthians 3:2-3 describes us as a _____ from Christ to be read by _____.

Titus 2:7 says that as teachers or leaders over others, we are to set an _____ by doing what is _____.

Our example should include what three things? _____, _____, and _____.

Pray: *Heavenly Father, show me how to be an example to others, to lead with integrity, so You can use me for the glory of Your kingdom. In Jesus' name I pray.*

Day 15

DAVID REFUSES TO HARM THE LORD'S ANOINTED

And he said to his Men, "The Lord forbid that I should do this thing to my master, the lord's anointed, to stretch out my hand against him, seeing he is the anointed of the Lord." (1 Samuel 24:6)

David refused to dishonor or harm the Lord's anointed, the one whom God had placed in authority, though he had several opportunities to do so (also see 1 Samuel 26:5-12).

Though he had been anointed to be the next king of Israel, in 1 Samuel 26:10 David told his men God would take care of removing Saul and moving him into leadership when God's timing was right.

Trusting God's plan and timing allows Him to orchestrate events to fulfill His purpose for our lives.

Drawing Closer to God

Psalm 61:7 says our _____ and our _____ depend only on _____.

Romans 12:2 warns us not to _____ to the _____ of the world.

In 1 Samuel 24:4, David's men tried to tempt him to _____.

1 Samuel 24:5 says David's conscience began to bother him because he _____.

Trusting God's perfect plan and timing allows us to set an example for those we lead and help them to also fulfill their destiny.

Pray: *Heavenly Father, I trust Your plan and Your timing in my life. Please strengthen me to follow only Your ways and not allow the world to interfere in Your plan for my life and those I lead. In Jesus' name I pray.*

Day 16

DAVID AND ABIGAIL

The name of the man was Nabal, and the name of his wife Abigail. ***And she was a woman of good understanding and beautiful appearance;*** *but the man was harsh and evil in his doings. He was of the house of Caleb.* (1 Samuel 25:3 emphasis added)

Abigail's wisdom and understanding saved her husband's life and in her own words kept David from needless bloodshed. "Let no wrongdoing be found in you…and you will not have on your conscience the staggering burden of needless bloodshed" (1 Samuel 25:28, 31 NIV). She was wise and beautiful inside and out. David married her after the Lord struck Nabal dead.

A beautiful woman that also possesses "good understanding" is a priceless asset to her husband.

Drawing Closer to God

Proverbs 31:25-26 says the wife of noble character is clothed with _____ and _____, and speaks with _____.

Proverbs 10:23 says a fool like Nabal finds pleasure in _____ _____, but a man of _____ delights in _____.

Abigail's wisdom and understanding kept David from _____.

Seek a spouse and friends who have good understanding and wisdom.

Pray: *Heavenly Father, grant me wisdom and good understanding, so that I allow You to deal with those who treat me wrongfully and not take matters into my own hands. Please send me friends that will guide me in righteousness. In Jesus' name I pray.*

Day 17

DAVID IN THE ARMY OF ACHISH

Then Achish called David and said to him, "Surely, as the Lord lives, you have been upright, and your going out and your coming in with me in the army is good in my sight. **For to this day I have not found evil in you since the day of your coming to me."**
(1 Samuel 29:6 emphasis added)

Though there were those who did not trust David because he was a Hebrew, no evil was found in David by his army commander, Achish.

The Apostle Peter instructs us, "As obedient children, do not conform to the evil desires you had when you lived in ignorance. But just as he who called you is holy, so be holy in all you do; for it is written: 'Be holy, because I am holy'" (1 Peter 1:14-16 NIV).

No evil was found in David.

Drawing Closer to God

David truly strove to be a man after God's own heart no matter where he was or who he was with.

It is amazing that this foreign leader declared he had found no evil in David.

Though we may feel this is impossible for us in today's world, 2 Peter 1:3-4 tells us, God's divine nature has given us everything we need for a life of _____ and we can escape the corruption of the world caused by _____ _____.

What gives us this power over evil temptations?
_____

Pray: *Heavenly Father, help me to be holy like You are holy. Purge all evil from within me and send Your Holy Spirit to guide me in all righteousness. In Jesus' name I pray.*

Day 18

DAVID IS FAIR WITH HIS SOLDIERS

"Oh no, my brothers!" said David as he broke up the argument. "You can't act this way with what God gave us! God kept us safe. He handed over the raiders who attacked us. Who would ever listen to this kind of talk? The share of the one who stays with the gear is the share of the one who fights—equal shares. Share and share alike!" From that day on, David made that the rule in Israel—and it still is. (1 Samuel 30:23-25 MSG)

David used wisdom with those under his leadership. He called them brothers and gave orders to all his soldiers to share in the spoils regardless of their role in his army.

David had the heart of God and was fair to all of his soldiers.

He declared, "We are going to share equally. This backup army is just as important as those who went to the battlefront.

Drawing Closer to God

When David saluted those 200 men, he was telling them, "Well done! This victory is as much yours as it is of those who went out. You were useful right where you were. As your king, I declare that you are to share equally in the spoils of victory."

Read of the importance of all the parts of the Body of Christ in 1 Corinthians 12:12-26.

This says there should be no _____ in the Body of Christ.

David was saying every member of his army was
_____

How is this going to change your relationships at work, in your neighborhood, in your community, in your church, and in your family? _____

Pray: *Heavenly Father, grant me wisdom in my work, all my relationships, and my business affairs. In Jesus' name I pray.*

Day 19

KING DAVID GREW STRONGER AND STRONGER

*Now there was a long war between the house of Saul and the House of David. But **David grew stronger and stronger**, and the house of Saul grew weaker and weaker.* (2 Samuel 3:1 emphasis added)

God was with King David, and his kingdom and influence began to grow. His kingdom grew stronger and stronger while Saul's influence grew weaker and weaker.

David grew stronger and stronger as he diligently strove to be obedient to and serve God.

The Apostle Paul dealt with this by saying a battle rages within us as the Spirit is in conflict with the desires of the sinful nature. As we are led by the Spirit, we grow stronger and stronger and the pull of the sinful nature grows weaker and weaker.

Drawing Closer to God

Galatians 5:16 says if we live by the _____ we will not gratify the _____ of the _____.

Galatians 5:24 reminds us that if we belong to Christ then the sinful nature has been _____.

Galatians 5:8 warns about the law of _____ and _____.

How do we grow stronger and stronger?
_____

Pray: *Heavenly Father, I ask You to help my spirit grow stronger and stronger and my flesh to grow weaker and weaker. Show me what seeds I have been sowing that I should not. Show me the good seeds I should begin to sow. In Jesus' name I pray.*

Day 20

David's Reign Begins

David was thirty years old when he began to reign, and he reigned forty years.
(2 Samuel 5:4)

David's reign began at the age of thirty and lasted forty years. He was anointed by Samuel the prophet to be king over Israel when he was a teenager. Then it took years of training and trusting God before he officially received the throne as King over Israel at the age of thirty.

God's promises always come to pass, but in His timing not ours.

Many of the psalms of David reflect his journey from shepherding his father's sheep to the shepherding of the Father's people. He learned patience and to trust in the Father to become the leader God designed him to be.

Drawing Closer to God

One of these is Psalm 40. Read the whole psalm and choose the key points that bring encouragement to you as you wait patiently for the Lord. This will get you started:

"I waited patiently for the Lord and He _____ _____.

He lifted me out of _____.

He put a new _____ in my mouth.

Many will see and put their _____ in the Lord.

_____ is the man who puts his trust in the Lord.

Pray: *Heavenly Father, help me to be patient and put my trust in Your timing for all of Your promises to me. In Jesus' name I pray.*

Day 21

DAVID DANCED WITH ALL HIS MIGHT

*Then **David danced before the Lord with all his might**; and David was wearing a linen ephod. So David and all the house of Israel brought up the ark of the Lord with shouting and with the sound of the trumpet.* (2 Samuel 6:14-15 emphasis added)

David danced and there was loud shouting, music, and celebration. David knew how to celebrate with jubilance. This is a far cry from how some Christians celebrate God's presence on Sunday morning at church.

David celebrated God's presence with joy.

O come, let us sing to the Lord; let us make a joyful noise to the Rock of our salvation! Let us come before His presence with thanksgiving; let us make a joyful noise to Him with songs of praise! (Psalm 95:1-2 AMP)

Drawing Closer to God

Psalm 98:4 we are instructed to, make a _____ _____ to the Lord, and break forth and _____ for _____.

Psalm 98:6 adds, we should _____ _____ before the Lord, the King.

Read Psalm 100.

In verse 1 it says we are to _____ for _____ to the Lord.

In verse 2 we are told to _____ the Lord with _____ and come before His presence with _____.

Verse 4 exhorts us to enter His gates with _____ and His courts with _____.

Pray: *Heavenly Father, I ask You to give me a jubilant heart that I would truly celebrate Your presence with joy and thanksgiving. In Jesus' name I pray.*

Day 22

God's Greatness

Therefore You are great, O Lord God. For there is none like You, nor is there any God besides You, according to all that we have heard with our ears. (2 Samuel 7:22)

David was now the king, but he did not forget that it was God who promoted him and gave him the victories over his enemies. He continued to take the time to go and sit before God and openly declared God's greatness. "There is none like You, nor is there any God besides You."

David sat in God's presence and declared God's greatness.

He continued to lead by example and desired to serve God as he was instructed to do. He wanted to make sure the people worshipped and served only the one true God.

Drawing Closer to God

If we take the time to look around us, there is no doubt what a great and wonderful God we serve. Having been a shepherd boy and working outside the majority of his youth, David had come to appreciate the beauty of the world God had created.

As he grew into manhood and became a leader among his own people, he also witnessed God's greatness in protecting and guiding him into victory over his enemies.

Many of his psalms reflect his awe and appreciation for the greatness of the God he faithfully continued to serve as King.

Psalm 19:1 says the heavens _____ _____.

Psalm 24:1 declares _____.

Pray: *Heavenly Father, I believe in Your greatness and know there is none like You. In Jesus' name I pray.*

Day 23

The Lord Preserves David

And the Lord preserved David wherever he went. (2 Samuel 8:14)

The Lord preserved David wherever he went and continually gave him the victory over his enemies. The Lord preserved David through all his military campaigns.

He preserveth the souls of His saints; He delivereth them out of the hand of the wicked. (Psalm 97:10 KJV)

God preserves His people.

There was no doubt in anyone's mind that God was with David. God continued to not only deliver David from those who would come against him, God also gave David the victory over them.

Drawing Closer to God

David continued to give God the glory and left us his beautiful psalms to tell us how to have God preserve us as well.

Psalm 31:23 encourages us to _____ because the Lord _____ the faithful.

Psalm 116:6 explains that the Lord _____ those with _____ faith.

Psalm 145:20 promises the Lord preserves all those who _____ Him, but all the wicked will He _____.

Pray: *Heavenly Father, I come to You with child-like faith and ask You to keep me and preserve me wherever I go. In Jesus' name I pray.*

Day 24

DAVID AND MEPHIBOSHETH

Now David said, "Is there still anyone who is left of the house of Saul, that I may show him kindness for Jonathan's sake. (2 Samuel 9:1)

David remembered his best friend, Jonathan, who died with his father, Saul, in battle against the Philistines. Jonathan had a son, Mephibosheth, who was lame in his feet.

So David said to him [Mephibosheth], *"Do not fear, for I will surely show you kindness for Jonathan your father's sake, and will restore to you all the land of Saul your grandfather; and you shall eat bread at my table continually."* (2 Samuel 9:7)

David showed kindness to Mephibosheth out of love for his best friend Jonathan.

Drawing Closer to God

Though it was customary in those days for the king of a new dynasty to completely massacre anyone connected with the prior dynasty, David went against that principle and asked what he could do for the family of his best friend Jonathan. He chose kindness over tradition. David's kindness to Mephibosheth is a wonderful example of God's grace to us.

Read Paul' advice to his young disciple Timothy in 2 Timothy 2:24-26 as he sends him to oversee the church at Ephesus.

Why should a leader be kind to everyone?
_____

How is a godly leader to treat those who oppose him?
_____

Why? _____

Pray: *Heavenly Father, I ask You to help me show kindness to all those I come in contact with, even those who oppose me. In Jesus' name I pray.*

Day 25

DAVID AND BATHSHEBA

> *It happened in the spring of the year, at the time when kings go out to battle…, but David remained at Jerusalem….One evening David arose from his bed and walked on the roof of the king's house.* **And from the roof he saw a woman bathing, and the woman was very beautiful to behold.**
> (2 Samuel 11:1-2 emphasis added)

David stayed in Jerusalem in his palace when his army went out to battle. The story of David and Bathsheba is a sordid story of lust, adultery, and murder. David committed adultery with her, and she got pregnant. To hide his sin, David had her husband, Uriah, sent to the battle front and ordered the other soldiers to withdraw. Uriah was killed so now King David was also guilty of murder.

Being in the wrong place at the wrong time can produce incredible tragedy.

Drawing Closer to God

In Psalm 119, David writes, "Blessed are those whose ways are _____, who walk according to the laws of the Lord.

Blessed are those who keep his _____ and seek him with all their _____

They do no _____ but follow his _____.

[God has] laid down precepts that are to be _____ obeyed. Oh, that my ways were _____ in _____ your [God's] decrees!

Then I would not be put to _____ when I consider all [God's] _____. (1-6 NIV)

Pray: *Heavenly Father, I pray You keep me in the place You have ordained for me. Let me not deviate from the path You have chosen for me or compromise what I know You have commanded in Your Word. In Jesus' name I pray.*

Day 26

King David and the Prophet Nathan

Then the Lord sent Nathan to David…
(2 Samuel 12:1)

King David thought he had gotten away with his cover-up. However, God is aware of everything that goes on in the Earth and sent His prophet, Nathan, to confront David about his sin. The Prophet Nathan tells David the story of a greedy, rich man who takes the poor man's only lamb instead of taking a lamb from his own flock of many. King David is enraged and wants to punish the rich man. Then Nathan tells him he is the man.

Nathan was making a comparison of David, the rich man and Uriah, the poor man. David had many wives, but Uriah had only one wife, Bathsheba. David stole another man's wife and had the man killed. After he was confronted by the Prophet Nathan, King David admits he sinned against the Lord.

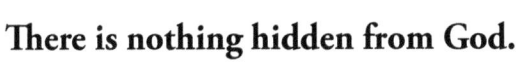

There is nothing hidden from God.

Drawing Closer to God

In Psalm 32:3-5, David shares what life was like with unconfessed sin in it:

When I refused to confess my sin, my body _____ _____, and I groaned ___ ___ long. Day and night [God's] hand of _____ was heavy on me. My _____ evaporated like water in the summer heat.

Finally, I _____ all my sins to [God] and stopped trying to _____ my guilt. I said to myself, "I will _____ my rebellion to the LORD." AND YOU [GOD] _____ ME! ALL MY GUILT IS _____."

(Psalm 32:3-5 NLT)

In Luke 8:17, Jesus warned us _____
_____

Pray: *Heavenly Father, I ask You to help me in confessing and repenting of my sin. In Jesus' name I pray.*

Day 27

God's Judgement on King David

Thus says the Lord: Behold, ***I will raise up adversity against you from your own house****; and I will take your wives before your eyes and give them to your neighbor, and he shall lie with your wives in the sight of this sun.* ***For you did it secretly, but I will do this thing before all Israel, before the sun.***
(2 Samuel 12:11-12 emphasis added)

God judges King David for his sins of adultery and murder. King David went through much heartache and misery caused by his own household. David could have been spared all of this torment had he not given into his lust over lovely Bathsheba.

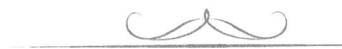

Sin has temporary pleasure, but in the end brings devastating consequences.

Drawing Closer to God

Read 2 Samuel chapters 12 and 13. Though David confessed and repented of his sin, there were still consequences of his sin.

It is so important to consider the long range affect our sin could have on our families before we give in to temptation and sin.

Proverbs 3:5-7 gives us guidance in how to stay on God's paths and avoid sin.

Trust in the _____ with all your heart,
And lean not on your own _____;
In _____ _____ _____ acknowledge Him,
And He shall _____ your paths.

Do not be _____ in your own eyes;
_____ the LORD AND DEPART FROM _____.

Pray: *Heavenly Father, remind me daily of the consequences of sin. I acknowledge You in all my ways, please guide me in Your ways that I might not sin against You. In Jesus' name I pray*

Day 28

KING DAVID HEARTBROKEN AT ABSALOM'S DEATH

> *Then the king was deeply moved, and went up to the chamber over the gate, and wept. And as he went, he said thus: "O my son Absalom—my son, my son Absalom—if only I had died in your place! O Absalom my son, my son!"* (2 Samuel 18:33)

King David was heartbroken over the death of his son Absalom. Even though Absalom had stolen David's throne and tried to kill him, David still loved his son.

Children sometimes treat their parents with contempt and disgust, but the parents still l ove them nonetheless, just as God our heavenly Father loves us nonetheless.

> *Consider the kind of extravagant love the Father has lavished on us—He calls us children of God!* (1 John 3:1 VOICE)
>
> *Most of all, love each other steadily and unselfishly, because love makes up for many faults.* (1 Peter 4:8 VOICE)

Drawing Closer to God

Those we love the most are often the ones who wound us the most and are also harder to forgive. God's love for us is unfailing. He not only forgives us when we disappoint and hurt Him with our actions, He chooses to forget them as well.

Read Psalm 103:11-18.

What do these verses tell you about God's love for you, your parents, and your children?

_____

_____

Pray: *Heavenly Father, take me, hold me, and guide me in forgiveness of every wrong my children have committed against me. In turn, I choose to forgive my parents of every wrong they have committed against me. Thank You, heavenly Father for Your great unconditional love for me. In Jesus' name I pray.*

Day 29

THREE YEARS OF FAMINE

Now there was a famine in the days of David for three years, year after year; and David inquired of the Lord... (2 Samuel 21:1)

When King David asked the Lord the cause of the famine, the Lord answered, "It is because of Saul and his bloodthirsty house, because he killed the Gibeonites," (2 Samuel 21:1). David went to the Gibeonites to make things right, and it ended the famine. This shows how we can be affected by the sin of others. The whole nation of Israel was undergoing a famine because of the actions of the previous king (Saul). However, if we inquire of the Lord, He will give us wisdom to deal with such generational curses.

The sin of others can affect us, however, if we humble ourselves and pray, God will forgive and heal us.

Drawing Closer to God

Read 2 Chronicles 7:14.

What do you need to do to deal with the effects of the sins of others in your life?

___

What's God's promise to you if you obey 2 Chronicles 7:14? (See Jeremiah 32:38-41.)

___

Read Joshua's challenge to God's people in Chapter 24:14-15.

How will you choose? _____

Pray: *Heavenly Father, fill me with wisdom in dealing with my sin and the effects of the sin of others in my life. As for me and my house, we choose to serve You. In Jesus' name I pray.*

Day 30

DAVID'S SONG

And he said: "The Lord is my rock and my fortress and my deliverer; the God of my strength, in whom I will trust; My shield and the horn of my salvation, My stronghold and my refuge; My Savior, You save me from violence. I will call upon the Lord, who is worthy to be praised; So shall I be saved from my enemies..." (2 Samuel 22:2-4)

David sang a song to the Lord after he was delivered from Saul and all his other enemies. The Lord put this song in David's heart by divine inspiration. The Lord will still do this today if we ask Him. Ask the Lord to put a song in your heart, then sing it out loud and clear.

Sing to the Lord the praises God puts in your heart as He brings to your remembrance His great love for you.

Drawing Closer to God

A psalm is a song. As we read through the psalms of David, we can clearly see God continued to give David new songs. It brings God joy when we sing out the songs He places in our hearts. Let what is your heart overflow into song. See what a difference it can make in your life.

Psalm 40:3 says, _____

Psalm 149:1 encourages us to sing a

_____

Ephesians 5:19-20 reminds us to

_____

Pray: *Heavenly Father, put a new song in my heart that I might overflow with love for You and sing to You the praises You deserve as I give You thanks for everything. In Jesus' name I pray.*

Day 31

DAVID NUMBERED THE PEOPLE

David's heart condemned him after he had numbered the people. So David said to the Lord, "I have sinned greatly in what I have done; but now, I pray, O Lord, take away the iniquity of Your servant, for I have done very foolishly." (2 Samuel 24:10)

Counting the number of people he reigned over was in this case a foolish act of pride for King David. David confessed and repented of his sin, but he still had to endure the consequences of his sin. We can ask forgiveness and repent of our sin, still have our eternal salvation, but the earthly, temporal consequences remain.

For instance, God will forgive you of a crime such as drunken driving or robbing a bank, but when you are caught by the cops, you still go to jail and serve your sentence.

God forgives the eternal consequences of sin through the atoning death of Jesus, but we will still have to face the temporal consequences of our sin.

Drawing Closer to God

Pride can be a very destructive problem if we do not keep it in check. David apparently taught his son, Solomon, about the dangers of pride as this wise man wrote many proverbs dealing with the issue of pride.

Proverbs 11:2 says when pride comes, then comes _____.

Proverbs 13:10 adds, by pride comes nothing but _____.

Proverbs 16:18 warns us, pride comes before _____. A haughty spirit before a _____.

In Proverbs 29:23, he says, a man's pride will bring him _____.

Pray: *Heavenly Father, help me recognize and repent of any pride or arrogance in my life. In Jesus' name I pray.*

Day 32

DAVID ADVANCED IN YEARS

Now King David was old, advanced in years; and they put covers on him, but he could not get warm. (1 Kings 1:1)

According to 1 Kings 1:1-4, in King David's later years he could not stay warm. David was suffering from the effects of aging just like everyone else. In our later years during declining health, we really have to continue to trust the God we have learned to serve throughout our lifetime.

Though our earthly bodies grow older, our love and trust of the Lord should still be apparent in our lives as we finish the race set before us.

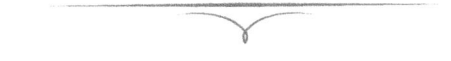

As for me, my life has already been poured out as an offering to God. The time of my death is near. I have fought the good fight, I have finished the race, and I have remained faithful. (2 Timothy 4:6-7 NLT)

Drawing Closer to God

"Do more than exist, live. Do more than hear, listen. Do more than agree, cooperate. Do more than talk, communicate. Do more than grow, bloom. Do more than spend, invest. Do more than think, create. Do more than work, excel. Do more than share, give. Do more than decide, discern. Do more than consider, commit. Do more than forgive, forget. Do more than help, serve. Do more than coexist, reconcile. Do more than sing, worship. Do more than think, plan. Do more than dream, do. Do more than see, perceive. Do more than read, apply. Do more than receive, reciprocate. Do more than choose, focus. Do more than wish, believe. Do more than advise, help. Do more than speak, impart. Do more than encourage, inspire. Do more than add, multiply. Do more than change, improve. Do more than reach, stretch. Do more than ponder, pray. Do more than just live, live for Jesus."[3]

Pray: *Heavenly Father, as my years advance, help me to always trust in and continue to serve You. In Jesus' name I pray.*

---

[3] John Mason, from his book, *You Can Do It — Even if Others Say You Can't*

Day 33

ADONIJAH TAKES THE THRONE

So Nathan spoke to Bathsheba the mother of Solomon, saying, "Have you not heard that Adonijah the son of Haggith has become king, and David our Lord does not know it? (1 Kings 1:11)

The throne belongs to Solomon, but his brother Adonijah decides he wants to take the throne instead. The prophet Nathan goes to Bathsheba to make sure God's choice for king, his son Solomon, receives the throne.

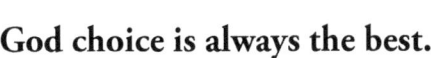

God choice is always the best.

Choosing to do things God's way always leads to God's best in our lives. This does not mean we make our own plans and then try to get God to agree with us. We are to seek Him first and do things His way. Then we receive the best He has in mind for us.

Drawing Closer to God

There are times when God's way does not seem logical to us, but when we choose to do things in His way and in His timing, God can bring us His very best.

Read Genesis 26:1-6 and 12-13.

What was going on in the land? _____

What did God instruct Isaac to do?
_____

What did God do for Isaac because he obeyed God's instructions? _____

Why is it so important to seek God's choices before making important decisions? _____

Pray: *Heavenly Father, help me to know and obey Your will for my life. In Jesus' name I pray.*

Day 34

David Charges Solomon

> *Now the days of David drew near that he should die, and he charged Solomon his son, saying: "…and keep the charge of the Lord your God: to walk in His ways, to keep His statutes, His commandments, His judgments, and His testimonies, as it is written in the Law of Moses, that you may prosper in all that you do and wherever you turn."*
>
> (1 Kings 2:1-3)

King David charges his son, Solomon, to keep the commandments of God. David had learned the importance of keeping God's commandments and knew if his son followed these instructions it would bring prosperity to him and to the kingdom he was called to rule.

Obeying God always brings prosperity, while disobeying God always brings a curse.

Drawing Closer to God

Read Deuteronomy 6 where Moses warns the Israelites about the importance of obeying God's commands as they enter their Promised Land.

What did Moses tell them they would receive if they obeyed God's commands?
_____

What did he warn them would happen if they did not?
_____

Verses 24 says if they obey they will _____ and be kept _____.

Pray: *Heavenly Father, I ask You to help me to always be obedient to Your commands that I may prosper and fulfill all that You have called me to do in my Promised Land. In Jesus' name I pray.*

Day 35

KING DAVID DIES

So David rested with his fathers, and was buried in the City of David. The period that David reigned over Israel was forty years; seven years he reigned in Hebron, and in Jerusalem he reigned thirty-three years. Then Solomon sat on the throne of his father David; and his kingdom was firmly established. (1 Kings 2:10-12)

King David died after a forty-year reign and lots of family drama. The affair with Bathsheba brought much trouble to his household. He was far from perfect, but he had a heart after God and repented of his sin.

Solomon receives his father's throne and asks God to give him a discerning heart to govern God's people and distinguish between right and wrong (1 Kings 3:7-9).

Drawing Closer to God

Solomon realized he needed God's help to truly lead God's people so he prayed for and received wisdom and discernment. Solomon shared what he learned in a collection of writings called Proverbs.

Proverbs 1:1-7 lists why Solomon wrote these proverbs. List what you will gain by studying these proverbs:

A good way to glean from Solomon's wisdom is to read and meditate on one Proverb every day. Keep a journal of what God reveals to you as you seek His wisdom and discernment on a daily basis.

Pray: *Heavenly Father, help me to have a heart that follows after You like King David. Forgive my sin and imperfections and give me a discerning heart to be the leader You have called me to be and to clearly distinguish between right and wrong. In Jesus' name I pray.*

Day 36

DAVID'S SOUL THIRSTS FOR GOD

O God, You are my God; **Early will I seek You; My soul thirsts for You;** *My flesh longs for You in a dry and thirsty land where there is no water. When I remember You on my bed, I meditate on You in the night watches.* (Psalm 63:1, 6 emphasis added)

Psalm 63 was written by David when he was in the wilderness of Judah. David was a seeker of God. He sought Him out early in the morning. The soul of David was "thirsty" for God. "Thirsty for God" is how we all should be no matter what is happening around us.

David suggests seeking God early in the morning and then reviewing and praising Him at the close of each day.

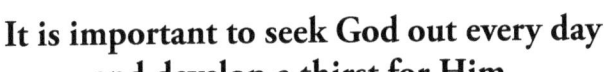

It is important to seek God out every day and develop a thirst for Him.

Drawing Closer to God

David had learned that by beginning each day in God's presence, it helped set his focus of his day.

Keeping a journal of your time in God's presence each day will help you stay on His course and help you with your daily decisions.

Ending each day remembering all you were able to accomplish with God's guidance and help reinforces the importance of your daily time with Him.

Take time at the end of each day to review your day and praise God for all His favor and provision.

Pray: *Heavenly Father, I ask You to help me in developing a thirst for Your presence early in the morning and praising You for Your provision at the end of each day. In Jesus' name I pray.*

Day 37

DAVID REPENTS WITH A CONTRITE HEART

*The sacrifices of God are a broken spirit, a **broken and a contrite heart**—These, O God, You will not despise.* (Psalm 51:17 emphasis added)

David wrote this psalm after Nathan the prophet confronted him concerning his adultery with Bathsheba. David was truly sorry and approached God with a broken spirit, and a broken and contrite heart.

The Forerunner Commentary SAYS BROKEN SPIRIT means "to be overwhelmed with sorrow." The Merriam-Webster Dictionary defines contrite as a feeling of remorse for a sin or shortcoming. A mature Christian does not make excuses, but admits he has sinned.

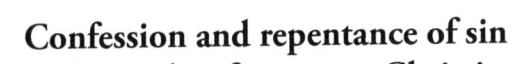

Confession and repentance of sin are the marks of a mature Christian.

Drawing Closer to God

Human nature is such that we tend to want to make excuses or qualify our sin as not as bad as someone else's.

Maturity means taking personal responsibility, admitting our sin, saying we are sorry, and determining how we can avoid repeating the same mistake again.

Psalm 38:18 says, I _____ my _____ and am _____ by my sin.

Repentance is more than saying we are sorry, it requires what? _____

2 Corinthians 7:10 says repentance leads to _____ and leaves no _____.

Pray: *Heavenly Father, I confess my sin to You right now with a contrite and repentant heart. In Jesus' name I pray.*

Day 38

DAVID ASKS GOD FOR A CLEAN HEART

__Create in me a clean heart, O God__, and renew a steadfast spirit within me. Do not cast me away from Your presence. And __do not take Your Holy Spirit from me__. (Psalm 51:10-12 emphasis added)

David asked God for a clean heart, and he pleaded with God not to take His Holy Spirit away from him even though he had sinned with Bathsheba and had her husband murdered.

There are times in our lives when we think we have done too much and gone too far that God can no longer use us in His kingdom work.

God's love for us never changes and once He cleans us up, He uses our testimony to draw others to Him.

Create in me a Clean Heart.

Drawing Closer to God

The Apostle Paul is great example of how God can take "the worst of sinners" and use them for His glory.

In 1 Timothy 1:12-16, read what Paul wrote to Timothy about God's love and grace.

Verses 12-13 say God considered Paul _____ and appointed Paul to His _____ even though Paul was a _____, _____, and a _____.

Verse 16 says Paul considered himself the

_____ of _____ to be an _____ of God's grace and mercy so others might _____ and receive _____ _____ because of Paul's testimony.

Pray: *Heavenly Father, I ask You to create a clean heart in me and show me how I can serve You in spite of my mistakes in life. In Jesus' name I pray.*

Day 39

DAVID WALKS IN GOD'S TRUTH

Teach me Your way, O Lord; **I will walk in Your truth**; *Unite my heart to fear Your name.* (Psalm 86:11 emphasis added)

Psalm 86 is a prayer from David. In verse 11, David asks God to teach him His way. Then David says he will walk in His truth.

David's next request is for God to unite his heart. This speaks to the struggle we all go through, even as Christians. We have the choice between God's way and our way. The choice between serving the Spirit and serving our flesh.

In Matthew 6:24, Jesus said man cannot serve two masters. We cannot serve God on Sunday and the world the rest of the week.

We learn God's way by praying and reading and studying the Bible. Then we must follow-up the Bible study with obedience and walk in that truth.

Drawing Closer to God

In order to walk in truth and truly serve God the way we should, we need an undivided heart that focuses on God's ways.

Jeremiah 32:39 says if we ask God, He will give us _____ of _____ and _____, so we will _____ Him, for our own _____ and for the _____ of our _____ as well.

In Ezekiel 11:19-20, God says He will give us an _____ heart and put a _____ _____ in us, and even remove our _____ of _____. Again this is because we need this to be able to _____ His _____.

Pray: *Heavenly Father, I ask You to teach me Your way and put an undivided heart and a new spirit in me that I may be obedient to Your laws. My heart's desire is to serve only You in all that I do. In Jesus' name I pray.*

Day 40

Your Word I Have Hidden in My Heart

How can a young man cleanse his way? By taking heed according to Your word. With my whole heart I have sought You; Oh, let me not wander from Your commandments! **Your word I have hidden in my heart, that I might not sin against You.** (Psalm 119:9-11 emphasis added)

David learned that the only way to live a clean, holy life without sin was to seek to know God's Word and then choose to obey it. We have His written Word the Bible. We must read and study it on a daily basis as we live our lives in a world that constantly seeks to draw us away from God's ways.

We need to learn from the examples and truths in God's Word to truly have a heart after God.

I will read Your Word and hide it away in my heart, so that I will not sin against You.

Drawing Closer to God

Apostle Paul's letter to the Christians in Colosse in Colossians 3:12-17 gives us a great list of ways to begin hiding God's Word in our hearts and draw closer to Him.

1. We are to clothe ourselves with: _____, _____, _____, _____, _____.

2. _____ each other.

3. We are to put on _____ which will being _____.

4. We are to let the _____ of God rule in our _____ and be _____.

5. We are to let the _____ of God _____ in us as we _____ one another.

6. Whatever we do and say, we are to do it _____.

Pray: *Heavenly Father, help me live a clean and holy life. Give me a hunger for Your Word, help me obey it as I seek to say and do everything to Your glory. In Jesus' name I pray.*

Conclusion

We have learned much from David's life over the last 40 days. The New Testament says these things were written for our benefit so we could learn and take warning.

> *These things happened to them as examples for us. They were written down to warn us who live at the end of the age.* (1 Corinthians 10:11 NLT)

Sin has its consequences. God's man, King David, was a mighty warrior, a great king, and a man after God's own heart. However, the consequences of his sin with Bathsheba brought him much grief and heartache for many years. Let us learn from David's mistakes. Let us also learn from the things he did right.

It is my prayer that this 40-day devotional has brought you closer to God.

Pray: *Heavenly Father, I humbly but boldly come before Your throne of grace. I give all my heart to You. I give all my desires to You. I hold nothing back. I ask You to fill me so full of the Holy Spirit that when people look into my eyes they see Jesus looking back. Help me not to judge people who are different than me, but help me to show Your love to all people everywhere I go. In Jesus' name I pray.*

Statement of Faith

I believe that one God exists in three persons: Father, Son, and Holy Spirit. Jesus Christ is the one and only Son of God who died for our sins and arose from the dead (1 Corinthians 15:1-8). The Bible is the inspired Word of God–a lamp unto our feet and a light unto our path (2 Timothy 3:16). Every person has worth as a creation of God, but all have sinned and fallen short of the glory of God (Romans 3:23). Forgiveness of sins and the promise of eternal life are available to those who trust Christ as Savior and Lord (John 3:16). The church is the body of Christ on earth, empowered by the Holy Spirit, and it exists to save the lost and edify the saved (Ephesians 4:1-16). Jesus Christ will one day return to earth and reign forever as King of kings and Lord of lords (1 Thessalonians 4:13-18).

Appendix

The Abigail Blessing

The name of the man was Nabal, and the name of his wife Abigail. ***And she was a woman of good understanding and beautiful appearance****; but the man was harsh and evil in his doings.* (1 Samuel 25:3 emphasis added)

Abigail was married to a very rich man named Nabal. He owned three thousand sheep and one thousand goats, but he lacked wisdom and understanding. He was harsh and evil. In fact, his name, Nabal, means "fool."

Abigail was very beautiful and her wisdom and understanding saved the lives of her husband and his servants.

Nabal had his men shearing his sheep when David entered the picture. David sent ten young men to ask for food from him. Nabal basically said, "Who does this David think he is?" Then he foolishly, refused to give any food to David's men.

When David heard about this, he gathered his army to attack Nabal and his household. David's plan was not to leave one male of all who belong to the house of Nabal.

When Abigail was told how foolishly her husband acted, she anticipated what might result from his actions. She made haste and took much food to David and his men. Abigail seized the information given, understood what needed to be done, and then did it.

When Abigail saw David, she dismounted quickly from her donkey and fell facedown before David and bowed to the ground. She asked for forgiveness for foolish Nabal and his household.

Abigail's plea brings an immediate positive response from David. We see David's instant gratitude, first to God and then to Abigail. David recognizes the hand of God in this situation. He praises this wise woman for taking action to stop him from causing innocent bloodshed. Except for her intervention, the obliteration of Nabal and his household would surely have been the result. She stood in the gap protecting both parties.

David said to Abigail, "Blessed is the Lord God of Israel who sent you this day to me, and blessed is your advice as you have kept me this day from coming to bloodshed and from avenging myself with my own hand."

In verse 35, David accepts the provisions from Abigail and instructs her to go home in peace telling her she had nothing to fear from him. David wisely heeds her words and request, choosing to allow God to take care of the situation with her husband.

After ten days, the Lord did indeed take care of foolish Nabal and he died of an apparent heart attack. When David heard of this, he proposed marriage to Abigail and she accepted.

Abigail's life with David would not always be easy. Instead of living in an established home in one location, Abigail becomes part of a group who moved from place to place avoiding the forces of Saul. Abigail was sent by God to help and support David on his journey to the throne.

It is interesting to note that Nabal was a fool, and yet he was still wealthy and rich. It is very possible his wealth and riches were due in part to Abigail's intervention in his business affairs.

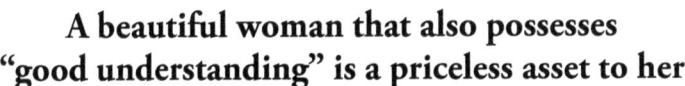

A beautiful woman that also possesses "good understanding" is a priceless asset to her husband. This is the Abigail Blessing.

How many men would love to have a wife like Abigail? She was beautiful. She was sensible. She was practical. She had great wisdom and understanding. This is indeed the Abigail Blessing. Proverbs 31:10-31 is a description of a wife whose value is beyond that of the rubies and precious gems. This type of wife is also as rare as a precious gem.

Proverbs 31:11 states, "The heart of her husband safely trusts her; so he will have no lack of gain. She does him good and not evil all the days of her life." Further down the chapter, the Proverbs 31 wife is described as a rising early to prepare food and make clothes for her household.

Proverbs 31 also states she has good business sense. She considers a field and buys it and from the profits plants a vineyard. Verse 23 states, "Her husband is known in the gates when he sits among the elders of the land."

Proverbs 31:28 also states the rewards of being this type of wife and mother. "Her children rise up and call her blessed; her husband also, and he praises her." Verse 30 says, "Charm is deceitful and beauty is passing, but a woman who fears the Lord, she shall be praised."

This describes the perfect wife. How many wives would fulfill all these qualities? It would seem to be almost impossible. However, it appears Nabal's wife Abigail did have all of these qualities. She was an example of the Proverbs 31 wife.

David recognized these qualities in Abigail and quickly proposed marriage to her because he knew she would be an asset to him.

It is interesting to note that a woman named Pauline Phillips, who wrote under the pen name, Abigail Van Buren, became a very popular advice columnist. According to Wikipedia, her parents were immigrants from Russia and also were Jewish. So, it is evident that she chose the biblical name Abigail as her pen name because Abigail was noted for being sensible and insightful.

Abigail Van Buren, also known as "Dear Abby," is very well known for her practical advice on a variety of subjects.

David's son Solomon could have learned to be practical and sensible by observing the understanding and wisdom of his step-mother, Abigail.

We all can learn from her and pray for the Abigail Blessing for our lives.

Pray: *Heavenly Father, grant me wisdom and "good understanding." Help me to be practical, sensible, and insightful. In Jesus' name I pray.*

About the Author

The author currently resides in Big Spring, Texas. He has a Master of Science degree from Hardin-Simmons University and is a Family Nurse Practitioner. He has two children and two grandchildren. He attends a non-denominational charismatic church in Big Spring, Texas. He has been involved in two medical missionary trips to Honduras, two medical mission trips to Mexico, and a construction mission trip to Peru. He has also been involved in various Men's and Children's Ministries over the years.

To write the author or to schedule speaking engagements, please E-mail him at: markmark_318@hotmail.com or call him at 432-213-6099.

Also check out Mark Sundy's book, "MAN OF GOD: *Fulfilling Your Destiny as a Man.*"

A Man of God is any man who delights in God's will and walks in the light of His truth, following in the footsteps of the Savior. This book will guide you in finding your own answers and becoming God's man!

www.ingramcontent.com/pod-product-compliance
Ingram Content Group UK Ltd.
Pitfield, Milton Keynes, MK11 3LW, UK
UKHW022215230426
12048UKWH00016BA/863